T0128193

Signs

of

Wellbeing

Marie Louise Devitt,
BSc, PGDip, MSc

BALBOA.
PRESS

A DIVISION OF HAY HOUSE

Balboa Press books may be ordered through booksellers or by contacting:

Balboa Press
A Division of Hay House
1663 Liberty Drive
Bloomington, IN 47403
www.balboapress.com
1 (877) 407-4847

Print information available on the last page.

ISBN: 978-1-9822-2992-4 (sc)
ISBN: 978-1-9822-2994-8 (hc)
ISBN: 978-1-9822-2993-1 (e)

Library of Congress Control Number: 2019908433

Balboa Press rev. date: 07/17/2019

Contents

Introduction

Hi, and welcome to *Signs of WellBeing*. I'm Marie Louise Devitt, and I am a wellbeing life coach and therapist. I'm Irish, but over the last thirty years, I have lived and worked in different countries in Europe and America. I now live in the United Kingdom with my second husband, and between us, we have five children or, rather, young adults. I have been divorced, been a single mom, and have had to restart my life three times in the last three decades. I also made the decision to go to university in my thirties to explore my passion for psychology. This led to me getting my degree, a postgraduate diploma in therapy and master's in the space of seven years. Through all of these life experiences, I have worked to support myself and my personal growth and development.

All these life experiences have certainly contributed to my life journey. They have also, more importantly, contributed to my ever-growing sense of curiosity about what really makes us, as humans, content and what feeds our souls. All these life experiences have enabled me to develop a deeper awareness of what steps I need to take on a daily basis to support myself. Taking these steps have helped me feel grounded and supported while maintaining my own inner sense of wellbeing and equilibrium.

I have become deeply passionate about supporting people in finding their own inner senses of wellbeing. I know from my experiences that this is within everyone's reach. Accessing it takes a little time, perseverance, and the application of a few fine-tuned skills. Developing a deeper level of awareness helps create deeper personal knowledge, and with this new knowledge comes the possibility and opportunity to change.

So join me as I walk you through the simple steps and perspectives that will help you achieve this. They will support you in living life on your terms and help you to genuinely feel at peace with who you are now, where you are now, and what you would like your future plans to look and feel like.

Chapter 1

The Secret to Content Living

I have often wondered what it would feel like to be truly content. I have always wanted to learn all that I could about what we, as individuals, need to do to feel content. Over time, I began to realize that it's not one specific thing that will make us content; it is a combination of things. When these things are brought together in balance, they support us in feeling content, at peace, and able and willing to experience our emotions in a fluid, empowering way.

This balance enables us to experience life in the here and now and on our terms. It also enables us to be fully present in our day-to-day lives. This sense of balance can also be described as a sense of wellbeing. Wellbeing is becoming a highly researched subject, and there is a range of theories and frameworks that focus on how to achieve this state. Interestingly, one theory that was put forward by the American psychologist Rhyffs acknowledges the importance of six specific areas that contribute to people's sense of wellbeing. These include:

- Self-acceptance (self-love and self-care)
- Personal growth (being able to step out of your comfort zone)
- Purpose in life (why you do what you do)
- Living life mastery (a feeling of "You've got this!")
- Autonomy ("I know my own mind and have a clear sense of myself.")
- Secure relations with others ("I'm at ease with my relationships and easily able to express myself.")

All these things, when combined in the right balance for each individual, will positively contribute to that person's sense of wellbeing. It is important to acknowledge that the balance of those six areas will potentially be different for each of us. It is about recognizing the perfect balance that works for you personally without being influenced by external factors, such as what your partners think, what your extended family might think, or what your friends might think. Some factors may be more important for some individuals than for others. And that is okay. There is no right or wrong in this regard. It is about finding the balance that resonates with you—balance that sits comfortably with you and resonates with who you truly are.

By helping yourself develop a deeper awareness of these wellbeing markers, you can learn how to manage them effectively. This then supports you in finding your individual state of equilibrium. So we have six markers to explore and consider. As you work to find the combination of these markers that fits best for you, think for a moment and consider these markers. Which of these are the most important for you personally?

What if applying these supportive steps around these six markers helped get you from a chaotic pace of life to a place of inner calm? Getting to know your wellbeing markers, reflecting on them, and tending to them regularly will help you feel more empowered. You will have your own go-to personal wellbeing system which will enable you to take life in your stride and stay grounded within your own sense of inner calm. So take some time to reflect, and consider what the most important markers are for you. Then think about what markers you would like to work on.

The Wellbeing Markers that Are Important for Me

_____

_____

_____

_____

_____

_____

_____

_____

_____

_____

_____

_____

The Wellbeing Markers that Are Important for Me

_____

_____

_____

_____

_____

_____

_____

_____

_____

_____

_____

_____

_____

The Wellbeing Markers that Are Important for Me

_____

_____

_____

_____

_____

_____

_____

_____

_____

_____

_____

_____

Chapter 2

Willingness to Reflect

*D*eveloping your reflective skills and adapting to a reflective state of mind will support you in creating a deeper awareness of the state of your wellbeing markers. Reflective skills help you identify those markers that may need tending to. This process involves allowing yourself to check in with yourself each day and reflect on the different aspects of your day, including what emotions you have felt and why. You can acknowledge what you did well, consider what situations you would like to have handled differently, what parts of your day you are grateful for, and what parts were a struggle for you. These reflections provide you with the information you need to assess your needs and areas for potential growth and to proactively support yourself in maintaining your ongoing sense of wellbeing.

Adapting to a reflective state of mind initially takes time and effort, but like almost anything else, with practice it becomes second nature and a natural part of your day-to-day life. When you consider developing a reflective state of mind to support yourself, what things do you feel could potentially get in the way? What do you think you can do to manage those obstacles? Can you write those thoughts down? Can you identify the steps you can take to support yourself to develop a more reflective state of mind? What would those steps be? You can be as creative as you like with this process. You can write things down, you can draw images that resonate with you, and you can even cut out images and paste them in the next few pages. Be as creative as you like during this process if that is what feels right for you.

How to Take Time for Reflection and Manage Obstacles that Get in the Way

_____

_____

_____

_____

_____

_____

_____

_____

_____

_____

_____

_____

How to Take Time for Reflection and Manage Obstacles that Get in the Way

---

Chapter 3

Self-Acceptance

(Self-Love and Self-Care)

The curious paradox is that when I accept myself
just as I am, then I can change.

—Carl Rogers

Self-Acceptance

Self-acceptance is a powerful process. When used, it can create a new view of yourself. Self-acceptance is when you, as an individual, choose to accept who you are in this present moment. That includes accepting all the good parts of yourself, all the parts you like less about yourself, and the parts you wished you didn't have to deal with. Self-acceptance is loving all aspects of yourself unconditionally in the moment. It's about letting go of all the judgements we impose on ourselves, such as being too fat, not funny enough, not happy enough, and not friendly enough.

The important thing to remember here is that each of us has several judgements that are specific and personal to us. And the process of self-acceptance is about choosing to let go of those judgements. Self-acceptance is about consciously choosing to wipe our self-judging slates clean and work to accept ourselves fully as we are in this moment without the if-onlys and what-ifs.

So will you, over the next few days, be mindful of how you talk to yourself and observe what your inner chatter is like? Is it supportive or judgemental? Does it put pressure on you? How can you rephrase what your inner chatter says to be more supportive and nurturing?

In the space below, write some newly rephrased chatter that will support you. Try applying this over the next three to five days. Then write what this has felt like for you. Again, as you engage in your reflective process, be as creative as you like about how you record this for yourself. Write a poem, do a list, draw some images, cut out some pictures; employ any visual cues that inspire and motivate you.

Self-Acceptance and Rephrased Inner Chatter

_____

_____

_____

_____

_____

_____

_____

_____

_____

_____

_____

_____

_____

_____

_____

Self-Acceptance and Rephrased Inner Chatter

_____

_____

_____

_____

_____

_____

_____

_____

_____

_____

_____

_____

_____

Chapter 4

Self-Acceptance, Self-Care, and Self-Nurture

When we think of self-acceptance, self-care, and self-nurture, what are we actually referring to? For me, this process is very much about how well we support ourselves from within. How well do you know yourself, and what do you need to feel okay and be at ease? Do you have a positive attitude about yourself? Do you feel able to offer yourself some self-love? How would you rate your capacity to care for and nurture yourself? In particular, do you know when it is important to offer yourself that support, self-love, and nurturing?

Could you say, "I like most aspects of my personality and regularly know what I need and how to meet those needs"?

What stops you, or what gets in the way of you being able to say that?

What comes to mind when you read this? Write your thoughts down in the space provided.

What do you do currently to care for yourself? How do you accept yourself on a daily basis?

Add some action steps you could put in place to support you this week.

Again, as you engage in your reflective process, be as creative as you like about how you record this for yourself. Write a poem, create a list, draw some images, write a short story for yourself, or cut out some pictures of any visual cues that inspire and motivate you.

Self-Acceptance (Self-Love and Self-Care)

_____

_____

_____

_____

_____

_____

_____

_____

_____

_____

_____

_____

_____

_____

Self-Acceptance (Self-Love and Self-Care)

_____

_____

_____

_____

_____

_____

_____

_____

_____

_____

_____

_____

_____

_____

Chapter 5

Offering Ourselves Openness and Acceptance

By learning to accept and love ourselves for who we are in this moment, we open up the path for personal growth which will, in turn, empower and support us. The first step to openness is the willingness to explore all aspects of what makes us who we are. Taking those first steps into being more open can feel scary and uncomfortable. Facing those fears and feelings and reassuring yourself that you can take things one step at a time and at your own pace can ease the discomfort. Remember that learning to accept and love who we are right now enables us to see those aspects of ourselves that we would like to develop and grow more clearly. At the heart of self-acceptance is our capacity to be our own best supporter, who is always there, cheering us on.

What can you say to yourself each day to accept who you are right now? What would you like to hear? Can you plan to say that to yourself each day? Can you write those thoughts down? Look at them, read them, and take them in.

If you were to think for a minute about those aspects of yourself you wish to be different or would like to develop a deeper understanding of, what would those be? Write those down too.

Body Scan Log

When you wake up and open your eyes, before you even get out of bed, take 1-2 minutes to do a body scan. Starting at the top of the head, check in to see how you feel. Does your head feel heavy? Do you feel pressure behind the eyes? Does your nose feel stuffy? Is your mouth dry? Check in with the rest of your body and continue with your neck, shoulders, back, arms, belly, legs, and feet.

Day of the week:
Body scan results:
Energy level upon waking: High — Okay — Low — Deplorable

Day of the week:
Body scan results:
Energy level upon waking: High — Okay — Low — Deplorable

Day of the week:
Body scan results:
Energy level upon waking: High — Okay — Low — Deplorable

Text message to the universe: When will you start noting your progress on the Body Scan Log?

When you start to have fewer episodes with digestive problems and you start to smile more because you are in a better mood, yell less at the kids, fight less with your spouse, and feel more energetic, you know that the effects of less sugar are taking effect.

Less pain in the joints was a big one for me in addition to the ones above. The achiness in the knees, back, shoulders, and other inflamed areas can start to lessen and eventually disappear.

For women, less painful and quicker passing menstrual cycles are a great thing too. Sugar can cause periods to be more painful, last longer, and be heavier. Hard to believe but true.

You might also want to notice if you are able to focus more and have more mental clarity.

If you are not feeling any benefits, your body may need more time, or it could be that the side effects of the medicine you are taking are hindering the process (if you are on medication). There could be many reasons, but you can't go wrong with removing processed foods and substituting them with vegetables.

Enter what you notice in the Body Scan Log. A blank template can be found in Appendix B. The template has been kept simple, so it can be re-created by hand if it cannot be downloaded and printed from my website.

Openness and Acceptance

_____

_____

_____

_____

_____

_____

_____

_____

_____

_____

_____

_____

_____

_____

_____

Openness and Acceptance

_____

_____

_____

_____

_____

_____

_____

_____

_____

_____

_____

_____

_____

_____

Chapter 6

The Need for Self-Care

Taking time out to do things for ourselves can sometimes feel like a luxury and not something that we can give time to. Many a time, the reason we burn out is because we keep on going even when we are running on empty. Taking care of ourselves is one way of recharging so that we can keep going in our daily lives. Taking care of ourselves is not a luxury but an essential requirement. Consider your self-care as your own required Ministry of Transport (MOT). We need our cars to get us where we need to go nearly every day. Law mandates that we have a MOT test done. Self-care is our own personal MOT test, and we cannot keep going without re-energising, refuelling, or regenerating ourselves. Think about what would help recharge your batteries.

List below three things that would help you to re-energise and refuel. These can be things that you really enjoy doing, things that make you feel glad you have done them, things that you get lost in, or even as a starting point, things that you have always been curious about trying and haven't till now.

Again, as you engage in your reflective process, be as creative as you like about how you record this for yourself. Write a poem, do a list, draw some images, cut out some pictures, or use any visual cues that inspire and motivate you. How would you represent self-care visually? What does it look like for you?

My Self-Care

_____

_____

_____

_____

_____

_____

_____

_____

_____

_____

_____

_____

_____

_____

Things for Re-Energising and Recharging

_____

_____

_____

_____

_____

_____

_____

_____

_____

_____

_____

_____

Chapter 7

Take Care of Your Body

llow yourself to take time to think about what your body
needs. Allowing your body to rest and exercise in a way
that resonates with you is massively important. All aspects of
ourselves are linked—mind, body, and soul. So when we take
care of all these aspects, we feel more present and more at ease
with ourselves. What can you do to help take care of your body,
to allow your body to rest or exercise in a way that resonates
with you?

So think and consider what you feel would be a good
support for you physically. What would help you to allow your
body to physically de-stress and unwind? What are some of the
things that help you feel your body's tension ease? There are
many possibilities, including yoga, walking, getting more sleep,
meditating, or sitting and reading. These are things that help
your body be still for a time to slow your breathing and take some

physical rest. Another thing that benefits your body is exercise. What exercise do you enjoy? It could be something as simple as walking, cycling, running, swimming, or a team sport. What do you enjoy the most? This is also an important aspect of this— doing things you enjoy that also involve exercise, so the more you enjoy the activity, the less like exercise it feels. So maybe think about what your weekly exercise routine could look like. Choose things that you enjoy doing. Add those to your routine. See what that feels like; maybe even test out new things until you find something you enjoy and are comfortable doing.

Body and Soul Nurturing Activities

_____

_____

_____

_____

_____

_____

_____

_____

_____

_____

_____

_____

_____

_____

Chapter 8

Body Nurturing

*I*nterestingly, many times we fall ill after a period of high stress, excessive working, or a combination of both. Most people will try to persevere and carry on regardless. If you were to think about it, how many times have you gotten ill like this? And when you reflect on the time leading up to the illness, were you coping with a lot of different things that were tiring for you both physically and mentally? Developing a deeper sense of awareness of how we feel physically is a really effective way of taking care of ourselves. Do you give yourself time to physically relax, allow your body to recharge, and give your body the best nutrients to support it? What do you do to take care of your physical self?

Body and Soul Rejuvenation and Relaxation

Things to Do to Take Care of My Physical Body

_____

_____

_____

_____

_____

_____

_____

_____

_____

_____

_____

_____

_____

Chapter 9

Take Care of Your Soul

*N*ow when I say "soul", I don't mean it in a religious way, and I fully respect the many perspectives and belief systems that exist. What I mean when I say "your soul" is your very special and individual essence. So what do you do to feed your soul? What are your passions? What things do you love the most? What are the things you can get lost in and come away from feeling totally relaxed and revived? Those are the things that feed and tend to your soul.

Taking care of your body and soul feeds into your sense of wellbeing and reduces your level of stress. Both need love and attention. Rest and relaxation lead to rejuvenation. What do you currently do to rejuvenate? What recharges your body and soul? Reflect on this for a moment, and then write down three to five things that will support the nurturing of your body and soul.

Body and Soul Rejuvenation and Relaxation

_____

_____

_____

_____

_____

_____

_____

_____

_____

_____

_____

_____

_____

Take time to do what makes your soul happy.

—Unknown

Chapter 10

Your Personal Support System

When you feel overwhelmed and stressed, think about what you can do for yourself to de-stress. Create a list of things you feel will support you in relaxing and de-stressing. This will be different for everyone, so that is why I ask you to think and create a support system that works best for you. Think back on times you felt stressed. What did you do in that situation to manage your stress? What helped to take your mind off the stressful situation? What actions helped you to alleviate the stress? Write these things down and create a visual reminder for yourself of the things that support you when you want to de-stress. Now, think about how you can use your support system this week. Even better, what if you used your system to support you even before you encountered stressful triggers or situations? Why not test that out for yourself? What would you like your support system to look like?

Write down all the things that could be included in your system.

Remember, no excuses. Having a support system in place is essential to feeling empowered in supporting yourself and maintaining your wellbeing.

_____

_____

_____

_____

_____

_____

_____

_____

_____

_____

_____

Your Personal Support System

_____

_____

_____

_____

_____

_____

_____

_____

_____

_____

_____

_____

_____

Chapter 11

Permission for Relaxation Time

Some people struggle to allow themselves to relax or to sit and rest. They constantly feel the need to be on the move or doing something. Relaxation time can take many forms. For everyone, it will be something that enables them to relax and unwind.

What does your ideal relaxation time look like? What would you be doing, and how would you be feeling? Now that you have that image, what do you need to do to make that happen? Relaxation time is a form of self-care. I encourage you to be kind to yourself; be your best supporter, not your worst critic. Allow yourself to rest and relax. It will help you in the long term.

Relaxation Time

_____

_____

_____

_____

_____

_____

_____

_____

_____

_____

_____

_____

_____

_____

Chapter 12

Space and Quiet

Finding time to give yourself some space and quiet will support you in working to quiet your mind and relax your body. Alone time is an important part of supporting yourself and reducing your stress. Giving yourself permission to be still and to rest and relax by giving yourself some space allows you to destress in a calm, natural way.

Stillness and quiet can be a struggle for us if we are used to being busy and feeling like we need to be doing something. And yet, if you give it a try, taking time for stillness, space, and quiet is a free and invaluable way to rejuvenate and reboot our bodies and souls.

So where do you think you can find that time and space to offer yourself the opportunity for stillness and quiet? At home sitting by the fire, sitting in your garden reading your favourite book, or being in the local park before the rush of people?

What comes to your mind as you think about possible locations? Write them down. And then, what can you do this week to offer yourself that space and quiet? Write down how you can plan that for yourself this week. Maybe put some time in your diary and call it "Space and Quiet." Do whatever will help you to actively commit and do this for yourself.

Space and Quiet

Chapter 13

Your Tranquil Space

Find a tranquil space that feeds your soul, and go there often.

*W*hat if you could find a place that really calmed you? What does that place look like in your mind? Is it somewhere you know? What draws you to that place? Think about these things, and see if you can replicate them in your home. Or find someplace nearby that gives you this. For some people, this may just be a walk by the sea; for others, a walk or hike outdoors. And for others, it may simply be the act of sitting calmly and reading their favourite books. So what is it that brings you peace and calm?

Knowing what supports us to relax and feel more tranquil gives us an essential resource to draw on when we feel we are approaching our limits or feeling drained and in need of some downtime.

Finding Tranquility: My Peace and Calm

_____

_____

_____

_____

_____

_____

_____

_____

_____

_____

_____

_____

_____

_____

Chapter 14

Meditation: Love It or Hate It

*I*ncreasingly in today's society, meditation is becoming a go-to method for people with a broad range of issues to support themselves. Meditation has also been well researched and regarded for its benefits, including the reduction of stress levels. If it is not something you have tried yet, do give it a go. It may initially take a little while to get used to sitting still and managing your thoughts, but if you allow yourself the time to stick with it and work to settle into the routine of meditation, it is a good tool that will help you to reduce your stress, clear your mind, and recharge your body. So why not give it a try?

In Meditation, it is possible to dive deeper into the mind to a place where there is no disturbance and there is absolute solitude. It is at this point in the profound stillness that the sound of the mind can be heard.

—A. E. I. Falconar

Considerations of Meditation

_____

_____

_____

_____

_____

_____

_____

_____

_____

_____

_____

_____

_____

Chapter 15

The Ripple Effect

Addressing and taking care of your personal needs and wishes give you a sense of fulfilment. In turn, you will feel more able and willing to give to people around you. Never underestimate the ripple effect of your change on the people around you.

In the space provided on the next page, write down what positive outcomes will occur in your life if you take better care of yourself and feel more energised and more at ease? What things would you do more happily and engage in, and how would people around you benefit from that?

Creating Your Ripple Effects

Creating Your Ripple Effects

_____

_____

_____

_____

_____

_____

_____

_____

_____

_____

_____

_____

_____

Before we move on to consider the marker of personal growth, think back on the things you have considered, and look at them in terms of improving your levels of self-acceptance, self-care, and self-nurturing. If you were to create three golden rules to support your ongoing state of self-acceptance, what would they be?

My Self-Acceptance Golden Rules

Personal Growth

Your vision will become clear only when you can look into your own heart. Who looks outside, dreams; who looks inside, awakes.

—Carl Jung

Chapter 16

Personal Growth

*P*ersonal growth can be defined as the willingness to continue to develop, grow, welcome new experiences, and recognise improvement in your behaviour and yourself over time.

Can you say, 'I think it is important to have new experiences that challenge how I think about myself and the world'?

Personal growth is also about being willing to step out of what feels familiar and comfortable, being willing to explore new things and new environments, and figuring out new aspects of yourself. It is about taking a deep breath and saying, 'Okay, I can do this.'

What aspects of your life do you wish to grow and develop? Would you like to have different or better relationships? Would you like to be able to bring yourself to your work in a different way? What personal growth questions do you ask yourself? Write them down here, and consider what you can do to work towards addressing those.

Again, as you engage in your reflective process, be as creative as you like about how you record this for yourself. Write a poem, do a list, draw some images, cut out some pictures, or use any other visual cues that inspire and motivate you. How would you visually represent your personal growth? What does it look like for you?

My Personal Growth Wishes

_____

_____

_____

_____

_____

_____

_____

_____

_____

_____

_____

_____

_____

_____

My Personal Growth Wishes

_____

_____

_____

_____

_____

_____

_____

_____

_____

_____

_____

_____

_____

_____

Chapter 17

Personal Power Empowers Us and Helps Us Grow

*P*ersonal power is about being able to trust your capacity to grow and develop, which enables you to step out of your comfort zone and try new experiences. These new experiences can challenge how you think about yourself and the world. Your personal power is what allows you to consider this new awareness and potentially integrate it into your view of yourself and the world. Feeling confident in your capacity to embrace new experiences and knowing that it will be okay open you up to new possibilities and experience. This process provides the opportunity for personal growth and helps you develop a deep sense of self-awareness, self-confidence, and self-worth.

Personal Strengths and Qualities

Personal Strengths and Qualities

Chapter 18

Personal Power Helps Us to Cope with Day-to-Day Life

*P*ersonal power also involves allowing yourself to look at those difficult experiences you have gone through, reflect on the experience, and work to acknowledge what you have taken from that experience. What was hard about that experience? How will that experience shape your approach to similar situations in the future? We learn from experiences as experiences feed our senses of personal power. And this is what helps us develop our resilience, coping strategies, and support systems.

What coping strategies do you use at the moment to support yourself? What do you do when you are having a difficult day? And how do you support yourself and work through what you are coping with? What personal strengths and qualities support you in times of stress and difficulties? What additional qualities would you like to develop or improve?

Personal Strengths and Qualities

_____

_____

_____

_____

_____

_____

_____

_____

_____

_____

_____

_____

_____

Chapter 19

Knowledge Is Key

*P*ersonal awareness and knowledge fuel personal growth. I can hear all the questions going through your mind right now: *How can I do this? How will this work?* Or, *But I have not done this before!* I am a big believer in the premise that with new knowledge and awareness comes the ability to change. So as you gradually work through this, considering the questions that have been put forth to you and reflecting on your answers, you will begin to understand yourself more deeply. You may even be able to identify some patterns that you have. With that awareness comes your ability to consider what aspects of your behaviour you would like to manage differently, while also working to change how you react and respond to situations going forward.

So believe that you can do this, and believe that you can do this on a daily basis. Tell yourself that every day. Simply say, 'It's okay. I've got this.'

Knowing others is intelligence, knowing yourself is true wisdom. Mastering others is strength. Mastering yourself is true power.

—Lao Tzu

Reflections—New Awareness

Reflections—New Awareness

Chapter 20

Growth and Reflection

*P*ersonal growth and reflection go hand in hand. Our capacities to use reflection skills enable us to look back over things, review what happened, and acknowledge the feelings that were felt, what was said, and what could have been said differently. It helps us consider things like how we acted and how we wish we had acted or responded? Reflections create new awareness for you and provide you with additional information to process and understand what actually happened and why on a deeper level.

You then choose how you use this new information. That is when your personal growth opportunity arises. So do you use this new awareness through reflection to inform how to handle these types of situations differently in the future? This would take you from a position of being reactive to situations to being more considerate and empowered in how and why you respond the way you do.

Growth through Reflections

Chapter 21

Capacity to Change

With personal growth and reflection comes the next step of choosing to change aspects of how we engage or do the things we do daily. How we respond and engage with change in our lives can be a challenge in itself, particularly if you are the type of person who struggles to cope with change of any sort.

Being aware of and testing how you feel about change will help you manage any potential blocks that may arise when you are working to choose to do or engage in things differently.

Think for a few minutes and consider how you respond to change. How do you manage your response to change? Would you like your response to be different? If so, how? Write down your thoughts on this. Also, consider how you might, over the next week, work to test out how you manage and respond to change.

Your vision will become clear only when you can look into your own heart. Who looks outside, dreams; who looks inside, awakes.

—Carl Jung

Feelings around Change

_____

_____

_____

_____

_____

_____

_____

_____

_____

_____

_____

_____

_____

_____

Chapter 22

Personal Accountability and Responsibility

*A*longside personal growth, reflections, and the capacity to change comes our willingness and openness to put our hands up and say, 'Yep, I need to be able and willing to change that aspect of my behaviour. I can see that it does not service me in the long term.'

Our capacity and willingness to look at ourselves, acknowledge all those aspects of ourselves, and be comfortable with the good and not so good put us in a strong position of being more willing to take full responsibility and accountability for our actions and behaviours. It is that personal accountability that will enable us to acknowledge those behaviours we could do with changing which, in turn, supports our personal growth and development.

Think about those parts of yourself or your behaviour that you can take responsibility for. How would you like to adapt or change them so that they serve you in a more effective way? What would those be? Write them down, and then list how you would like those aspects of yourself or your behaviour to be different and more helpful for you.

What do I know and own about myself and my behaviour? And how would I like those aspects of myself to be different going forward?

_____

_____

_____

_____

_____

_____

_____

_____

_____

_____

_____

What do I know and own about myself and my behaviour? And how would I like those aspects of myself to be different going forward?

_____

_____

_____

_____

_____

_____

_____

_____

_____

_____

_____

Chapter 23

Change as an Opportunity

An important aspect of personal growth is our capacity to cope with change. Learning to develop a positive relationship with change will support you in feeling more in control and more confident in your capacity to deal with change. Accept that change happens, and see change as a possible opportunity to develop, evolve, and grow. When we are coping with change, it is our abilities to adapt to change that are being tested. Change can take us out of our comfort zone and challenge us to mould and adapt to a new environment and way of doing things.

Be willing to consider change as a valuable opportunity to evolve and grow. What opportunities for change do you see for yourself? How would you like to see yourself manage this change? Write down your thoughts and hopes for handling these opportunities.

Change as Opportunity

Chapter 24

Personal Growth and Being Proactive

*A*nother aspect of personal growth is learning to overcome emotional blocks or things that we struggle to manage. Learning to allow ourselves to face those things head-on builds our confidence and promotes personal growth. For example, to reduce high levels of stress and manage it effectively going forward, we need to explore what causes those stressful feelings. One of the ways to manage your negative stress more effectively is by adopting a proactive approach to stress. Don't wait until you are completely stressed out. Think about your wellbeing marker of self-care. Work to address and manage your stress levels daily, and thus take care of yourself. To do that, you need to actively monitor how you are feeling. Know what your triggers are, be aware of your breathing and the tension in your body, and take time out from trigger situations. Take slow, calming breaths to recentre and get a clearer focus on what is going on for you.

Working towards addressing your stress may initially require some professional support. If you are struggling to understand what is causing it and how to manage your stress, seeking the support of a stress counsellor or life coach may be helpful. It may give you that start you need to effectively begin to manage your stress. The act of being proactive and willing to look at what you can do to support yourself in reducing your stress level is a crucial element of personal growth. It is part of our support system.

Can you think of what you could do to support yourself and be more proactively engaged in promoting your own wellbeing on a daily basis? What comes to mind? What would help you to do that for yourself?

How do I become more proactive
about my wellbeing?

_____

_____

_____

_____

_____

_____

_____

_____

_____

_____

_____

_____

How do I become more proactive
about my wellbeing?

_____

_____

_____

_____

_____

_____

_____

_____

_____

_____

_____

_____

_____

Everything that irritates us about others can lead us to an understanding of ourselves.

—Carl Jung

Reflections

_____

_____

_____

_____

_____

_____

_____

_____

_____

_____

_____

_____

_____

_____

Chapter 25

Learning to Choose Your Emotional State

*P*art of how being personally accountable supports us lies in the way it empowers us. It allows us to understand that we have the capacity to make our own decisions and, particularly, to make decisions about how to cope with our emotions and what emotions we choose to embrace on a daily basis.

Look for the joyous aspects of your life. What things are you grateful for? What are the things that you love in your life and you have around you? For example, nature, being with friends, family, or sport. Allow yourself to really enjoy and value these situations and events. Look for the positives in your life. Embrace those, and hold them close.

Remember, laughter and joy create positive psychological and physical benefits. So consider this. How often do you laugh? What can you do to bring more laughter into your life? Allow yourself to acknowledge those things that you love and are grateful for on a daily basis.

Write down all those things that you love and are grateful for in your life. Make this your gratitude and love list.

Gratitude and Love List

_____

_____

_____

_____

_____

_____

_____

_____

_____

_____

_____

_____

_____

_____

Gratitude and Love List

Chapter 26

Embrace Your Playful Side

*E*ven though you are a grown-up now, you are still allowed and encouraged to embrace your childlike, playful side. Allow yourself to have fun, dance, watch a funny movie, and have a laugh with friends. Embrace the positive energy that you get from that. Allow yourself to put the negatives to one side for a while. The break will do you good.

Create your playfulness activities list. What activity brings out your playful side? Think back to when you were younger. What were the things that made you laugh? What are the things that make you laugh now? What does your list look like? Which of those activities could you try out this week?

Laughter List

Laughter List

_____

_____

_____

_____

_____

_____

_____

_____

_____

_____

_____

_____

_____

_____

Before we move on to consider the marker of purpose in life, think back on the things you have considered. Look in terms of exploring potential things to promote your personal growth. If you were to create three golden rules to support your ongoing personal growth and development, what would they be?

My Personal Growth Golden Rules

_____

_____

_____

_____

_____

_____

_____

_____

_____

_____

_____

_____

_____

_____

Purpose in Life

When goals go, meaning goes. When meaning goes, purpose goes. When purpose goes, life goes dead on our hands.

—Carl Jung

Chapter 27

Purpose in Life: Why You Do What You Do

Knowing what one's life purpose is can be a big question to some people. And yet others know from the moment they can talk what it is they want to do or be in their lives.

Your purpose in life is grounded if you have a good foundational awareness of what your why is in life and what motivates you to do what you do. If you have a purpose in life, it helps you develop a strong goal orientation and conviction that life holds meaning.

Can you say, 'I have a clear understanding of my purpose in life and lead my life with that in mind'?

Why do I do what I do?

_____

_____

_____

_____

_____

_____

_____

_____

_____

_____

_____

_____

_____

Chapter 28

Choosing to Live by Your Values

Some people find it hard to unravel their life purposes. Nothing stands out for them as such to make it seem obvious. Some basic foundations of the life purpose can be identified clearly. For that, ask yourself these questions: What are your life values? What life principles do you live by?

For example, one person may care about supporting people and making a positive impact on other people's lives. That value can potentially influence someone while choosing a job in the caring profession. Someone who has a love for the outdoors and loves being among nature could choose to be a gardener, a nature-reserve warden, or some other job that involves working with land, nature, and the outdoors. So think and reflect about what you value in this world.

What is important to me? What are
my values and life principles?

_____

_____

_____

_____

_____

_____

_____

_____

_____

_____

_____

Chapter 29

Living by Your Why

*P*art of what informs our understanding of our life purposes is getting to know our whys. What motivates us to do what we do, why we go to work, and why we live where we live. There are some aspects in life where our choices may be limited, but in a situation where you have the capacity to make choices for yourself, you will tend to choose to live in a particular place for a particular reason. It may be because the area has good schools or because the geographical location is appealing to you. Likewise, you may choose a job because you like something about that type of work. So many of our life decisions have a why behind them.

Thinking about our life purposes can feel like a big question that is in front of us, and sometimes, it is a difficult one to answer. As for me, my life purpose is not just about one set thing. I sometimes look at it as my life vision—what I would like to see myself doing, who I would like to be seen with me while I do this, where we will be, and what the environment will look and feel like. And then I ask myself, 'Do my actions and the decisions I make on a daily basis support me in reaching this vision I have of myself?' This is my test question.

So what would you like your life vision to look like? How would you like to feel? What would you be doing? Who would be with you? And where would you be? Brainstorm this in the next few pages. Be as creative and free with this exercise as you can, and don't hold back. Give it 100 per cent, and see what you come out with. Also, stop and think for a moment. Would you like to have some additional whys or motivations in your life? If so, what would you like those to be?

Life Purpose and Life Vision

Life Purpose and Life Vision

_____

_____

_____

_____

_____

_____

_____

_____

_____

_____

_____

_____

_____

_____

The good life is a process, not a state of being. It is a direction not a destination.

—Carl Rogers

Where would you like your life
direction to take you?

Chapter 30

The Joy of Laughter

Sometimes we get caught up in the things that are not right about our day or our lives. We can lose sight of our life vision or life purpose. So it is important to work to keep a balance and find ways to see the positives in your life. Identify what those positives are, and remind yourself of them regularly while also being mindful of that life vision you have for yourself.

Allow yourself to see the brighter side of life. Remember, we can choose our emotional state. Laughter and joy create positive psychological and physical benefits. Remind yourself that 'A laugh a day helps keep your stress at bay.' I know this may seem hard to believe, but you can work to make a choice to be happy. Try it out for a day. Assign one day a week as your happy day. Be aware of how that feels, and think about what felt different about your happy day.

My Happy Day Experience

_____

_____

_____

_____

_____

_____

_____

_____

_____

_____

_____

_____

_____

Chapter 31

Re-Energising Yourself

As you go through your daily activities and responsibilities, your life vision and life purpose can seem distant and disconnected. Your day-to-day life can, at times, deplete your internal energy and drive resources. It is essential is to find ways that help re-energise and recharge your energy levels and your drive to live your daily life. This supports you towards living your life vision and life purpose. So think about what you can do for yourself that will achieve this. It will be different for everyone. For one person it could be something like taking the time to sit and read a good book, but for someone else, it may be going for a walk with friends out in nature, and for others, it may be being part of a club.

So what things can you do for yourself that you enjoy and get pleasure from? When was the last time you did something that helped you recharge? Creating a regular recharging routine for yourself promotes an overall sense of wellbeing in the long term, which releases new energies and motivations for you to tap into.

Re-Energising

Before we move on to consider the marker of living life masterfully, think back on the things you have considered in terms of developing a deeper awareness of your purpose in life. If you were to create three golden rules to support your ongoing commitment to your purpose in life, what would they be?

My Purpose in Life Golden Rules

_____

_____

_____

_____

_____

_____

_____

_____

_____

_____

_____

_____

_____

_____

_____

Day-to-Day
Life Mastery

With realization of one's own potential and self confidence in one's ability, one can build a better world.

—Dalai Lama

Chapter 32

Living Life Masterfully

*L*iving life masterfully is having the courage and confidence to make choices and decisions that support you in your day-to-day life, and it will greatly support your sense of wellbeing. This helps you be able to make effective use of opportunities and have a sense of mastery in managing everyday affairs and creating situations to benefit your personal needs. For example, in general, I feel like I am in charge of the situation in which I live.

So when you think about how you support yourself and take charge of the situation in which you live, think about what helps you do that. Can you name those things you do to support yourself on a daily basis to do that? Or if you feel you don't do that right now, would you like to be able to do that in the future? What do you feel you need to do differently?

My Living Life Mastery Strategies

_____

_____

_____

_____

_____

_____

_____

_____

_____

_____

_____

_____

_____

_____

_____

_____

Chapter 33

Setting Healthy Boundaries

Part of what mastering living our lives involves being aware of our personal boundaries in our daily lives and working to maintain them. By being able to manage and tend to those boundaries, we support ourselves and our senses of wellbeing. It is important to find a healthy balance between being there and giving all we have to the people around us and being able to give ourselves some time to rejuvenate, relax, and recharge.

We can only do so much for the people around us. Gaining the ability to say no and set healthy boundaries will empower you. It also makes space for you to do the things you genuinely wish to do. This then has the knock-on effect and makes you feel more willing and able to be there for people around you. If you could choose one boundary to put in place for yourself that would support you, what would it be?

What are my personal boundaries?

_____

_____

_____

_____

_____

_____

_____

_____

_____

_____

_____

_____

_____

_____

Chapter 34

Environmental Triggers

*P*art of mastering living our lives involves knowing how we are feeling and then managing and supporting ourselves through those feelings. In today's society, there are increasing reports about high levels of stress/anxiety and depression. One of the most important factors in addressing stress is the ability to actually acknowledge that you are feeling stressed. It is about being able to put up your hand and say, 'Actually, you know what? I am struggling with this, and I need some help.'

Once you have acknowledged what you are struggling with, you will be able to do something about it. Then you can work to master how you can best support yourself going forward. So be mindful of how you are feeling. Test your stress levels regularly and know what your okay is like. When you feel yourself shifting away from this okay, think about what is going on and what you can do to bring yourself back to that okay place.

Think about what your personal signs for being okay are. When you feel okay, what contributes to that for you? And then think about what things can upset the apple cart for you. What things can trigger you to get to a place of not being okay?

I know I am okay, when ...

_____

_____

_____

_____

_____

_____

_____

_____

_____

_____

_____

_____

_____

_____

Chapter 35

Managing My Stress Levels

When you feel your stress building, think about what would help you feel less stressed. How do you process those stressed feelings? How do you work to allow yourself to let those feelings go? And what do you do to recharge after you have been coping with a high level of stress? Draw on the support system you have. Use what you are most drawn to or feel you need the most. What might help you take your mind off things? What might help you relax physically?

What do I need?

_____

_____

_____

_____

_____

_____

_____

_____

_____

_____

_____

_____

_____

Chapter 36

Dealing with Change in Your Life

*D*ealing with change is stressful, particularly change that is outside your control. Work towards acceptance that there are things you cannot change while reminding yourself that you can control how you react and respond to this change. This will support you in reducing the stress of coping with change. Work to identify the things in that situation you can control and manage. What can you do? What can you directly impact? And how can you work to address those things directly?

Managing My Reactions to Change

Chapter 37

Being Proactive about Environmental Stressors

The only way to reduce your negative stress is to adopt a proactive approach to stress. Don't wait until you are completely stressed out. Address it daily. When I say stressed out, this can refer to a number of things depending on you as an individual. It may be that you are constantly tired and irritable, it may be that you are in a constant state of frustration about some person or thing, or it may be that you feel constantly overwhelmed. Think about how you feel. Are you feeling stressed out in one sense or another?

The first crucial step to addressing your stress is to acknowledge you are stressed. By acknowledging your stress levels, you can do things to address it, including seeking support, finding ways to relax, giving yourself some downtime, and finding things that help take your mind off your stress for a little while.

Coping with Day-to-Day Life Stressors

Chapter 38

Stressful Situations in Our Lives

What is the most stressful part of your day? Find someone supportive to talk things through with. Think about how you can support yourself to work through your stressful feelings, and then think about what would help you to let those feelings go. Knowing our stress triggers is a good first step to addressing those things that cause us stress. Moreover, thinking through how we would like to manage those triggers empowers and supports us.

Create a top-three list of trigger situations that cause you stress. Once you have your list, create some proactive support strategies that you feel will help you dealing with those situations more effectively.

Proactive Approaches to My Triggers

_____

_____

_____

_____

_____

_____

_____

_____

_____

_____

_____

_____

_____

Chapter 39

Your Living Life Mastery Support System

*H*aving an established support system that is there for you when you are struggling and feeling stressed is important and reassuring. Think about what you would like your support system to look like. It may include having a few go-to people whom you can call or talk to when struggling with something. It may include going to the gym, for a run, or to a yoga class to help you unwind. Perhaps spending time doing a favourite past-time or hobby, reading a book. Whatever it is that works for you to release your stress and feel more at ease.

Think for a little while about the people or activities that you have at your disposal. Then in the space provided on the next page, compile your stress-free support system. Be as creative as you like. This is your support system, so don't hold back. Try and list at least five things or people. Remind yourself of this support system when you feel like your stress is building. Which one would be first on your list? How do you feel now, looking at the support system you have created for yourself?

Living Life Mastery Support System

_____

_____

_____

_____

_____

_____

_____

_____

_____

_____

_____

_____

_____

Before we move on to consider the marker of autonomy, think back on the things that you have considered. Look in terms of what will support you to be the master of your environment. If you were to create three golden rules to support your ongoing personal growth and development, what would those be?

My Environmental Mastery Golden Rules

_____

_____

_____

_____

_____

_____

_____

_____

_____

_____

_____

_____

_____

_____

_____

Autonomy

Chapter 40

Autonomy

*Y*ou feel independent and can manage and cope with your behaviour independent of outside influences (societal). For example, I have confidence in my opinions even if they are different or go against the general consensus.

How comfortable are you being your own person, being an individual, and not one of the crowd?

My Sense of Myself

_____

_____

_____

_____

_____

_____

_____

_____

_____

_____

_____

_____

_____

_____

Chapter 41

Engaging with My Environment

Try not to let your fear of change stop you from doing those things you wish you could do. Think about how you can develop your own sense of independence and what that would feel like.

If you could choose one thing you would like to change in your life, what would it be? What would you gain if you changed this one thing? How would it feel once you made this change?

Engaging with My Environment

_____

_____

_____

_____

_____

_____

_____

_____

_____

_____

_____

_____

_____

_____

Chapter 42

Mastering Me and Then Mastering My Day-to-Day Living

We tend to put the needs and wishes of others first. When we do this, we can start to feel drained and frustrated. Choosing to take care of yourself is an important step in supporting yourself. Having a deeper connected sense of what you need and being independent enough to give that to yourself will promote your inner sense of wellbeing.

You can still be aware of the needs and wishes of others and work to meet those but in a more balanced way. Make an active decision to be kind to yourself, give yourself a break, take the pressure off yourself, and commit to this way of being wholeheartedly. That will be your gift to yourself. The key to managing this well is adjusting your mind-set to believe that it is okay to do things that support you. So don't hesitate. Don't judge yourself or go back and forth about whether or not it is okay. Giving yourself full permission to take care of yourself is a priceless gift.

What is one thing you could give yourself this week that would support you?

Mastering Me, Mastering My Day-to-Day Living

_____

_____

_____

_____

_____

_____

_____

_____

_____

_____

_____

_____

_____

_____

Chapter 43

Clearing Our Mental Clutter

One important thing that really supports our sense of self is being really clear about our positions on things and being able to live in ways that acknowledge those beliefs. When we have a lot of things on our minds, it is hard to feel clear about how we really feel about different aspects of our lives, what our needs are, and what the best choices are for us.

Working to clear out our mental clutter can help create some mental space to make room for new thinking and awareness. When the mind is cluttered, it is harder to get clarity about things. So how do we do a mental declutter? Say the thoughts out loud and talk things out. Even better, make a list of all the things that you are thinking about. Get them out of your head and on paper. Doing this on a regular basis helps clear your mind. If you feel confused and have a number of things on your mind, make a list of the things going through your mind, and rank them in importance.

Why don't you give it a go now? Write some of those recurring thoughts on the next page. Take the first steps to clearing your mental clutter.

My Mental Declutter

My Mental Declutter

_____

_____

_____

_____

_____

_____

_____

_____

_____

_____

_____

_____

_____

_____

Chapter 44

What Do You Feel You Need Right Now?

Sometimes it is worth taking a moment to reflect on how you feel and potentially identify what need. This helps you feel more grounded and less stressed. Then you can work out how you can give that to yourself. There is only so much we can expect from the people around us. We also need to support ourselves.

Your ability to say no and set your own healthy personal boundaries may well give you more room to think about what your needs are. As you go through this week, think about what you would love to give yourself—some rest, time with friends, a day out in nature, or some downtime. It's your choice. Then set apart some time in your diary to do this for yourself.

Be kind to yourself, and commit to it wholeheartedly.

Tell yourself that by giving you what you need, you will be less resentful of people around you and will feel more able and willing to care for and support them. By planning and committing to giving yourself some quality time, you are not only taking care of yourself but also the people around you.

What do I need right now?

_____

_____

_____

_____

_____

_____

_____

_____

_____

_____

_____

_____

_____

What do I need right now?

_____

_____

_____

_____

_____

_____

_____

_____

_____

_____

_____

_____

_____

_____

Chapter 45

Our Capacity to Say, 'Time Out'

One thing you can certainly do if you feel you are getting to the end of your tether, constantly tired, or feel your stress levels building is to allow yourself to take some time out. Think about how you can buffer those triggers to support your own wellbeing.

If you are in a stressful situation and feel your levels of stress building, excuse yourself politely and take a break. Step out of the stressful situation.

You are allowed to take care of yourself if you need to. So don't be afraid to give yourself even just ten minutes to gather and regroup yourself. Sometimes just a ten-minute break is all you need.

So can you identify some possible timeout options for yourself. How long could they be, what could you do, and where could you go? Create a plan for yourself; be prepared and willing to use it for yourself.

Possibilities for a Timeout

_____

_____

_____

_____

_____

_____

_____

_____

_____

_____

_____

_____

_____

_____

Before we move on to consider the marker of positive relationships, think back on the things that you have considered and in terms of exploring potential things to promote your autonomy. If you were to create three golden rules to support your ongoing deeper sense of self, what would they be?

My Sense of Autonomy Golden Rules

Secure Relationships

Health is the greatest gift, contentment the greatest wealth, faithfulness the best relationship.

—Buddha

Chapter 46

Secure Relationships

Another wellbeing marker is the capacity to have secure and positive relationships. When you are in a secure relationship, you can relate and interact with others in meaningful relationships that include reciprocal empathy, intimacy, and affection.

When you think about your relationships, what do you bring to the mix? What are your strengths in developing and maintaining secure relationships? When you think about your relationships, how comfortable are you in relating to the people with whom you have relationships? How would you rate your capacity to offer empathy, intimacy, and affection in your relationships?

Secure Relationships

_____

_____

_____

_____

_____

_____

_____

_____

_____

_____

_____

_____

_____

_____

Chapter 47

Negative Influences on Secure Relationships

egative influences that can impact and interfere with these secure relationships can include feelings of stress. If we feel stressed, we have less time to give to the people around us in our workplaces and homes. Additionally, we can sometimes take our stresses out on the people closest to us. Being mindful of our stress and tendency to take it out on the ones nearest and dearest to us gives us the ability to make a choice to not do so.

Being mindful of our stress levels also helps keep us more present in our lives. Choosing to actively not take those stressed feelings out on people around you supports those relationships more positively. Taking that more considerate approach to how you act and respond, while knowing what you want to give to and receive from your relationships, promotes your sense of wellbeing and naturally reduces stress levels.

What do you think you can do differently over the next week to be more mindful of your stress levels? What can you do differently this week so that you manage how you react and respond to the people around you when stressed?

Secure Relationships

_____

_____

_____

_____

_____

_____

_____

_____

_____

_____

_____

_____

_____

Secure Relationships

Chapter 48

Your Relationships and Your Expectations

When we are stressed or struggling with life, we can have high expectations of how people around us need should support and understand us. When they don't meet those expectations, we tend to get annoyed with them. And then we blame them.

Be mindful of pointing fingers at the people around you. The only actions and behaviours you can directly change are your own. Taking your stress out on the people around you will only add to your stress.

> Remember, you don't get what you don't ask for
> and no-one can mind read and know what your
> needs are, so please ask for what you need.

So as you think about your relationships now—and be really honest with yourself—what do you feel you could do differently? And how would this help you improve the quality of your relationships?

How would I like to improve my relationships?

_____

_____

_____

_____

_____

_____

_____

_____

_____

_____

_____

_____

Chapter 49

Feeling Connected to the People in Your Life

Feeling connected and engaged with the people around us supports our wellbeing. Being able to make time to pay attention and really listen to the people in our lives supports better relationships and a better understanding of what is going on for them.

Many things can get in the way of being able to give our full attention to the people around us. They include technology, paying attention to something else, or doing other things and not making time for the people in our lives.

How can I feel connected to people in my life?

_____

_____

_____

_____

_____

_____

_____

_____

_____

_____

_____

_____

_____

_____

Chapter 50

Developing Secure Relationships

To improve our relationships, we cannot point the finger at other people first. We can think about what we can do differently in the relationship that would support us in feeling more connected. The important point to be mindful of is that the only behaviour we can control or change is our own, not anyone else's. A starting point of this is making time and really being present in conversations or interactions that you have with the people around you.

Think for a moment, and then write down what things you would like to try to do differently to support you in making more time for the people around you and enable you to be more present when you are together.

Developing Deeper Connections

_____

_____

_____

_____

_____

_____

_____

_____

_____

_____

_____

_____

_____

_____

Chapter 51

Building Friendships for Wellbeing

*P*art of what supports your wellbeing is having friends that you feel comfortable to reach out to and who support you. Staying connected with people close to you supports your wellbeing. The friendship you proactively offer to the people around you also builds and maintains that sense of connection. Remember, you are a crucial element in this universe. You are here because you are important, and you count.

What do you love most about yourself? What qualities do you bring to your friendships? Remember to see your good qualities as strengths that you can use to support yourself. Also remember that nobody is perfect. We all have flaws. Your friends will not always meet your expectations. Remind yourself that we are all human, and no one is perfect. However, if the pattern continues, maybe it is worth talking about how you feel, sharing this with a friend, and seeing if he or she can take this on board. If that pattern doesn't change, you can choose how much time and energy you invest in this type of friendship. You can set your own boundaries about how you wish to be treated within friendships too. Having healthy friendship boundaries supports your inner sense of wellbeing.

What healthy friendship boundaries do you use to support yourself in your friendships?

Healthy Friendships for Wellbeing

Healthy Friendships for Wellbeing

_____

_____

_____

_____

_____

_____

_____

_____

_____

_____

_____

_____

_____

As we consider this final wellbeing marker of positive relationships, think back on the things that you have considered in terms of exploring potential things to promote your positive relationships. If you were to create three golden rules to support your ongoing commitment to your relationships, what would they be?

My Own Sense of Secure Relationship Golden Rules

_____

_____

_____

_____

_____

_____

_____

_____

_____

_____

_____

_____

Love is all we need.

—The Beatles

Chapter 52

Putting Love in Your Life

      inally, there's one important concept to consider. Love is a powerful thing. Allowing ourselves to bring love intentionally into how we engage in our day-to-day lives will strongly influence our states of wellbeing. Bringing love into our lives always starts with self-love. Identify one thing you could do differently to benefit both you and the people around you as you go through your day. Choosing to love ourselves can be a real challenge as it takes time and effort. Sometimes taking care of yourself is down to you. If you feel you need something from the people around you, you need to ask clearly for what you need. Remember, the people around you are not mind readers. If they cannot give you what you need, consider if it is something you can give to yourself. There is no limit to how much self-care and self-nurturing you can give to yourself.

Bringing More Love into My Life

Bringing Even More Love into My Life

Your Golden Rules for Maintaining
Your Six Wellbeing Markers

Finally, to recap and solidify where you have gotten to, list your golden rules for each of your markers below. Use these as your reminder when looking to refocus

Self-Acceptance

_____

_____

_____

_____

_____

Personal Growth

_____

_____

_____

_____

_____

Purpose in Life

_____

_____

_____

_____

_____

_____

Living Life Mastery

_____

_____

_____

_____

_____

_____

_____

Autonomy

_____

_____

_____

_____

_____

_____

Secure Relationships

_____

_____

_____

_____

_____

_____

The real person smiles in trouble, gathers strength from distress, and grows brave by reflection.

—Thomas Paine

Printed in the United States
By Bookmasters